Symphony No. 1
in C Major, Op. 21
&
Symphony No. 2
in D Major, Op. 36

Ludwig van Beethoven

• 1st or 3rd movement
intro / expo. / 2nd ending
• menuet
• all 7 clefs like middle...

DOVER PUBLICATIONS, INC.
Mineola, New York

Copyright

Bibliographical Note

This Dover edition, first published in 2001, is a republication of music from *Symphonies de Beethoven, partitions d'Orchestre,* originally published by Henry Litolff's Verlag, Braunschweig, n.d.

International Standard Book Number: 0-486-41399-3

Manufactured in the United States of America
Dover Publications, Inc., 31 East 2nd Street, Mineola, N.Y. 11501

Contents

Symphony No. 1
in C Major, Op. 21

Composed, 1800. First performance: 2 April 1800.
Dedicated to Baron Gottfried van Swieten

•

Symphony No. 2
in D Major, Op. 36

Composed, 1801–2. First performance: 5 April 1803.
Dedicated to Prince Karl von Lichnowsky

Instrumentation

2 Flutes [Flauti, Fl.]

2 Oboes [Oboi, Ob.]

2 Clarinets [Clarinetti, Cl.]
Sym. No. 1 = in C
Sym. No. 2 = in A

2 Bassoons [Fagotti, Fag.]

2 Horns [Corni, Cor.]
Sym. No. 1 = in C, F
Sym. No. 2 = in D, E

2 Trumpets [Trombe, Tr.]
Sym. No. 1 = in C
Sym. No. 2 = in D

Timpani [Timpani, Tp.]

Violins I, II [Violino]

Violas [Viola]

Cellos [Violoncello, Vc.]

Basses [Basso/i]

Symphony No. 1

in C Major, Op. 21

I

7
Fl.
Ob.
Cl.
Fag.
Cor.
Tr.
Tp.
ten. ten.
cresc.
Allegro con brio. 𝅗𝅥 = 112.
Allegro con brio. 𝅗𝅥 = 112.
Allegro con brio. 𝅗𝅥 = 112.
15
Fl.
Ob.
Cl.
Fag
Cor.
cresc.
tr

26
Fl.
Ob.
Cl.
Fag.
Cor.
Tr.
Tp
sf
ff
a 2.
36
cre
scen

44
Fl.
Ob.
Cl.
Fag.
Cor.
Tr.
Tp.
do.
ff
53
p
sf

63
Fl.
Ob.
Cl.
Fag.
Cor.
Tr.
a 2.
74

82
Fl.
Ob.
Cl.
Fag.
Cor.
Tr.
Tp.
a 2.
cresc.
91
Fl.
Ob.
Cl.
Fag.
Cor.
Tr.

100
Fl.
Ob.
Cl.
Fag.
Cor.
Tr.
Tp.
1.
2.
111

119
Fl.
Ob.
Cl.
Fag.
Cor.
Tr.
130
Fl.
Ob.
Cl.
Fag.
Cor.
cresc.

140
Fl.
Ob.
Fag.
148
Fl.
Ob.
Fag.

157
Fl.
Ob.
Cl.
Fag.
Cor.
Tr.
166
Fl.
Ob.
Cl.
Fag.
Cor.
Tr.

178
Fl.
Ob.
Cl.
Fag.
Cor.
Tr.
Tp.
a 2.
ff
sf
p
189
cresc.

198
Fl.
Ob.
Cl.
Fag.
Cor.
Tr.
Tp.
ff
sf
p
206
Fl.
Ob.
Cl.
Fag.
Cor.

217
Fl.
Ob.
Cl.
Fag.
Cor.
Tr.
Tp.
a 2.
a 2.
a 2.
227
Fl.
Ob.
Cl.
Fag.
Cor.
Tr.
Tp.

236
Fl.
Ob.
Cl.
Fag.
Cor.
Tr.
Tp.
cresc.
245

256
Fl.
Ob.
Cl.
Fag.
Cor.
Tr.
Tp.
sf
ff
p
265
cresc.
f

275
Fl.
Ob.
Cl.
Fag.
Cor.
Tr.
Tp.
ff
sf
285
a 2.

II

Andante cantabile con moto. ♪ = 120.
Flauto I.
Oboi.
Clarinetti in C.
Fagotti.
Andante cantabile con moto. ♪ = 120.
Corni in F.
Trombe in C.
Timpani in C. G.
Andante cantabile con moto. ♪ = 120.
Violino I.
Violino II.
Viola.
Violoncello e Basso.
Vcl.
pp
12
Fl.
Ob.
Cl.
Fag.
Cor.
Bassi.
cresc.
sf

24
Fl.
Ob.
Cl.
Fag.
Cor.
a 2.
Vcl.
Bassi.
38
Fl.
Ob.
Cl.
Fag.
Cor.
cresc.
cresc.
Vcl.
Bassi.

47
Fl.
Ob.
Cl.
Fag.
Cor.
Tr.
Tp.
a.2.
57
Fl.
Ob.
Cl.
Fag.
Cor.
Tr.
Tp.
cresc.
p cresc.

69
Fl.
Ob.
cresc.
Fag.
p cresc.
Cor.
79
Fl.
Ob.
Cl.
Fag.
Cor.
Tr.
Tp.

88
Fl.
Ob.
Cl.
Fag.
Cor.
Tr.
Tp.
a 2.
cresc.
99
Ob.
Fag.
cresc.
Vcl.
cresc.

108
Fl.
Ob.
Cl.
Fag.
Cor.
Bassi.
p
117
cresc.
sf
f

127
Fl.
Ob.
Cl.
Fag.
Cor.
Vcl.
Bassi.
140
Fl.
Ob.
Cl.
Fag.
Cor.
Vcl.
Bassi.

151
Fl.
Ob.
Cl.
Fag.
Cor.
Tr.
Tp.
162
Ob.
Cl.
Fag.
Cor.

174
Fl.
Ob.
Cl.
Fag.
Cor.
Tp.
pizz.
185
Fl.
Ob.
Cl.
Fag.
Cor.
arco

III

MENUETTO

28
Fl.
Ob.
Fag.
p
pp
cresc.
Bassi.
43
Fl.
Ob.
Cl.
Fag.
Cor.
Tr.
Tp.
a.2.
f
ff
sf

57
Fl.
Ob.
Cl.
Fag.
Cor.
Tr.
Tp.
cresc.
a 2.
71
TRIO

87
Ob.
Cl.
Fag.
Cor.
99
Ob.
Cl.
Fag.
Cor.

111
Cl.
Cor.
decresc.
pp
p
123
Fl.
Ob.
Cl.
Fag.
Cor.
Tr.
Tp.
a 2.
ff
sf
Men. D. C.

IV

Adagio. ♪ = 63.
Allegro molto e vivace. 𝅗𝅥 = 88.
Flauti.
Oboi.
Clarinetti in C.
Fagotti.
Corni in C.
Trombe in C.
Timpani in C.G.
Violino I.
Violino II.
Viola.
Violoncello e Basso.
ff
p
pp
8
Fag.
Vcl.

17
Fl.
Ob.
Cl.
Fag.
Cor.
Tr.
Tp.
cresc.
Bassi.
29
Fl.
Ob.
Cl.
Fag.
Cor.
Tr.
Tp.

40
Fl.
Ob.
Cl.
Fag.
Cor.
Tr.
a 2.
50
decresc.

61
Fl.
Ob.
Cl.
Fag.
Cor.
cresc.
74
Fl.
Ob.
Cl.
Fag.
Cor.
Tr.
Tp.

87
Fl.
Ob.
Cl.
Fag.
Cor.
Tr.
Tp.
1.
96
2.
Vcl.
Bassi.

107
a 2.
Fl.
Ob.
Fag.
ff
fp
p
Vcl.
Bassi.
120
sempre p
Basso .
Vcl.
129
Fl.
Ob.
Fag.
Cor.
p
a 2.
cresc.
Basso

139
Fl.
Ob.
Cl.
Fag.
Cor.
Tr.
Tp.
cresc.
a 2.
151

161
Fl.
Cl.
Fag.
p
168
Fag.
p
Vcl.
Bassi.
177
Fl.
Ob.
Cl.
Fag.
Cor.
Tr.
p
cresc.
f
a 2.
cresc.

189
Fl.
Ob.
Cl.
Fag.
Cor.
Tr.
decresc.
p
200
p cresc.
cresc.
sff
a 2.
f
sf

212
Fl.
Ob.
Cl.
Fag.
Cor.
Tr.
Tp.
224
a 2.
a 2.

236
Fl.
Ob.
Cl.
Fag.
Cor.
Tr.
Tp.
246
Fl.
Ob.
Cl.
Fag.
a 2.
Vcl.
Bassi.

257
Fl.
Ob.
Cl.
Fag.
Cor.
Tr.
Tp.
270
Fl.
Ob.
Cl.
Fag.
Cor.

280
Fl.
Ob.
Cl.
Fag.
Cor.
Tr.
Tp.
cresc.
p cresc.
a 2.
291

Symphony No. 2
in D Major, Op. 36

I

8
Fl.
Ob.
Cl.
Fg.
Cor.
Tr.
Tp.
p
sf
ff
sfp
cresc.
p cresc.
14

17
Fl.
Ob.
Fg.
Cor.
20
Fl.
Ob.
Cl.
Fg.
Cor.
Tr.
Tp.
cresc.

23
a. 2.
Fl.
Ob.
Cl.
a 2.
Fag.
Cor.
Tr.
Tp.
Vel.
Basso.
28
Fl.
Ob.
Cl.
Fag.
Cor.
Tr.
Tp.
cresc.
Bassi.

33
Ob.
Fg.
Cor.
Allegro con brio
cresc.
f
p cresc.
p
fp
Vcl.
Basso
Bassi.
6
39
Fl.
Ob
Cl.
Fag
Cor.
Tr.
Tp.
a 2.

48
a 2.
Fl.
Ob.
Cl.
Fag.
Cor.
Tr.
Tp.
56

64
Fl.
Ob.
a 2.
Fag.
a 2.
Cor.
a 2.
Tr.
71
Fl.
a 2.
Ob.
Cl.
Fag.
Cor.
Tr.
Tp.
Vcl.
Basso.
Bassi.

80
Fl.
Ob.
Cl.
Fag.
Cor.
Tr.
Tp.
p cresc.
p
ff
sf
Vcl.
Basso.
Bassi.
88
a 2.

96
Fl.
Ob.
Cl.
Fag.
Cor.
Tr.
Tp.
ff
pp
cresc.
106
Fl.
Ob.
Cl.
Fag.
Cor.
Tr.
Tp.
sf
ff
fp
a 2
tr

114
Fl.
Ob.
Cl.
Fag.
Cor.
Tr.
Tp.
a 2.
122
Fl.
Ob.
Cl.
Fag.
Cor.
Tr.
Tp.
a 2.

130
Fl.
Ob.
Cl.
Fag.
Cor.
Tr.
Tp.
1.
2.
Vcl.
140
cresc.

150
Fl.
Ob.
a 2.
Fag.
Cor.
Tr.
158
Fl.
Ob.
Fag.
Cor.
Tr.
Tp.
Basso.
Vcl.

165
Fl.
Ob.
Cl.
Fag.
a 2.
Cor.
a 2.
Tr.
Tp.
172
Fl.
Ob.
cresc.
Cl.
Fag.
Cor.
Tr.
Tp.
Vcl.

179
Fl.
Ob.
Fag.
pp
p
Bassi.
Vel.
189
cresc.
f
ff

198
Fl.
Ob.
Fag.
a 2
sf
206
Cor.
ff
p
p cresc.
cresc.

215
Fl.
Ob.
Fag.
Cor.
sf
p
cresc.
Vcl.
Basso.
Bassi.
223
Fl.
Ob.
Fag.
Cor.
p
cresc.

232
Fl.
Ob.
Fag
Cor
Tr.
Tp.
240
Fl.
Ob.
Cl.
Fag
Cor
Tr.
Tp.
Vcl.
Bassi.
Bassi.

250
Fl.
Ob.
Cl.
Fag
Cor
Tr.
Tp.
cresc.
Vcl.
Basso.
Bassi.
258
a.2.

266
Fl.
Ob.
Cl.
Fag
Cor
Tr.
Tp.
277
Fl.
Ob.
Cl.
Fag
Cor
Tr.
Tp.
cresc.
cresc.
cresc.
cresc.
tr

285
Fl.
Ob.
Cl.
Fag
Cor.
Tr.
Tp.
ff
fp
p
sf
293
ff

302
Fl.
Ob.
Cl.
Fag
Cor
Tr.
Tp.
cresc.
cresc.
cresc.
312
Fl.
Ob.
Cl.
a.2.
Fag
Cor
Tr.
Tp.

321
Fl.
Ob.
Cl.
Fag.
Cor.
Tr.
Tp.
334

343
a.2.
Fl.
Ob.
a.2.
Cl.
Fag.
Cor.
Tr.
Tp.
a.2.
a.2.
352
Fl.
Ob.
Cl.
Fag.
Cor.
Tr.
Tp.

II

Larghetto. ♪ = 92.
Flauti.
Oboi.
Clarinetti in A.
Fagotti.
Corni in E.
Larghetto. ♪ = 92.
Violino I.
Violino II.
Viola.
Violoncello e Basso.
Vcl.
Bassi.
Basso.
cresc.
12
Cl.
Fag.
Cor.
Vcl.

24
Cl.
Fag.
Cor.
cresc.
cresc.
cresc.
cresc.
Bassi.
35
Fl.
Ob.
Cl.
Fag.
Cor.
Vcl.
Bassi.

47
Fl.
Ob.
Cl.
Fag.
Cor.
cresc.
55
Vcl.
Bassi.

64
Fl.
Ob.
Cl.
Fag.
Cor.
a.2.
cresc.
75
Fl.
Ob.
Cl.
Fag.
Cor.
cresc.

82
Ob.
Cl.
Fag.
Cor.
Vcl.
Basso.
90
Fl.
Ob.
Cl.
Fag.
Cor.
Bassi.
cresc.
decresc.

99
Fl.
Ob.
Cl.
Fag.
Cor.
p cresc.
cresc.
p
107
f
pp

118
Fl.
Ob.
Fag.
pp
cresc.
f
128
ff
134
p
Vcl.

141
cresc.
Bassi.
148
Fl.
Ob.
Cl.
Fag.
in A.
Cor.
decresc.
pizz.
arco Vcl.
Basso.
163
Bassi.
arco.

172
Cl.
Fag.
Cor.
cresc.
Vcl.
Bassi.
183
Cl.
Fag.
Cor.
cresc.

194
Fl.
Ob.
Cl.
Fag.
Cor.
Vcl.
Bassi.
204
decresc
cresc.

216
Fl.
Cl.
Fag.
Cor.
Vcl.
Bassi.
cresc.
225
Fl.
Ob.
Cl.
Fag.
Cor.
a.2.
cresc.

236
Fl.
Ob.
Cl.
Fag.
Cor.
cresc.
245
Vcl.
Bassi.
Basso.

254
Fl.
Ob.
Cl.
Fag.
Cor.
Bassi.
cresc.
a.2.
decresc.
264

III

SCHERZO

Allegro 𝅗𝅥. = 100.
Flauti.
Oboi.
Clarinetti in A.
Fagotti.
Allegro 𝅗𝅥. = 100.
Corni in D.
Trombe in D.
Timpani in D.A.
Allegro 𝅗𝅥. = 100.
Violino I.
Violino II.
Viola.
Violoncello e Basso.
13
Fl.
Ob.
Cl.
Fag.
Cor.
Tr.
Tp.

25
Fl.
Cl.
Fag.
fp
pp
Vcl.
pp Basso.
35
Fl.
Ob.
Cl.
Fag.
Cor.
Tr.
Tp.
cresc.
f
p
ff
f Bassi.

47
Fl.
Ob.
Cl.
Fag.
Cor.
Tr.
Tp.
decresc.
decresc.
61
Fl.
Ob.
Cl.
Fag.
Cor.
Tr.
Tp.
cresc.
cresc.
cresc.
cresc.
cresc.
cresc.
cresc.
cresc.
Vcl.
Basso.
Bassi.
Vcl.
Basso.

74
Fl.
Ob.
Cl.
Fag.
Cor.
Tr.
Tp.
p cresc.
Bassi.
TRIO
90

98
Fl.
Ob.
Cl.
Fag.
Cor.
Tr.
Tp.
a.2.
p decresc.
pp
ff
115
pizz.
cresc.
Scherzando da capo.

IV

Allegro molto. (𝅗𝅥 = 152.)
Flauti.
Oboi.
Clarinetti in A.
Fagotti.
Corni in D.
Trombe in D.
Timpani in D. A.
Violino I.
Violino II.
Viola.
Violoncello e Basso.
Vcl.
Bassi.
Basso.
9
Fl.
Ob.
Cl.
Fag.
Cor.
Tr.
Tp.

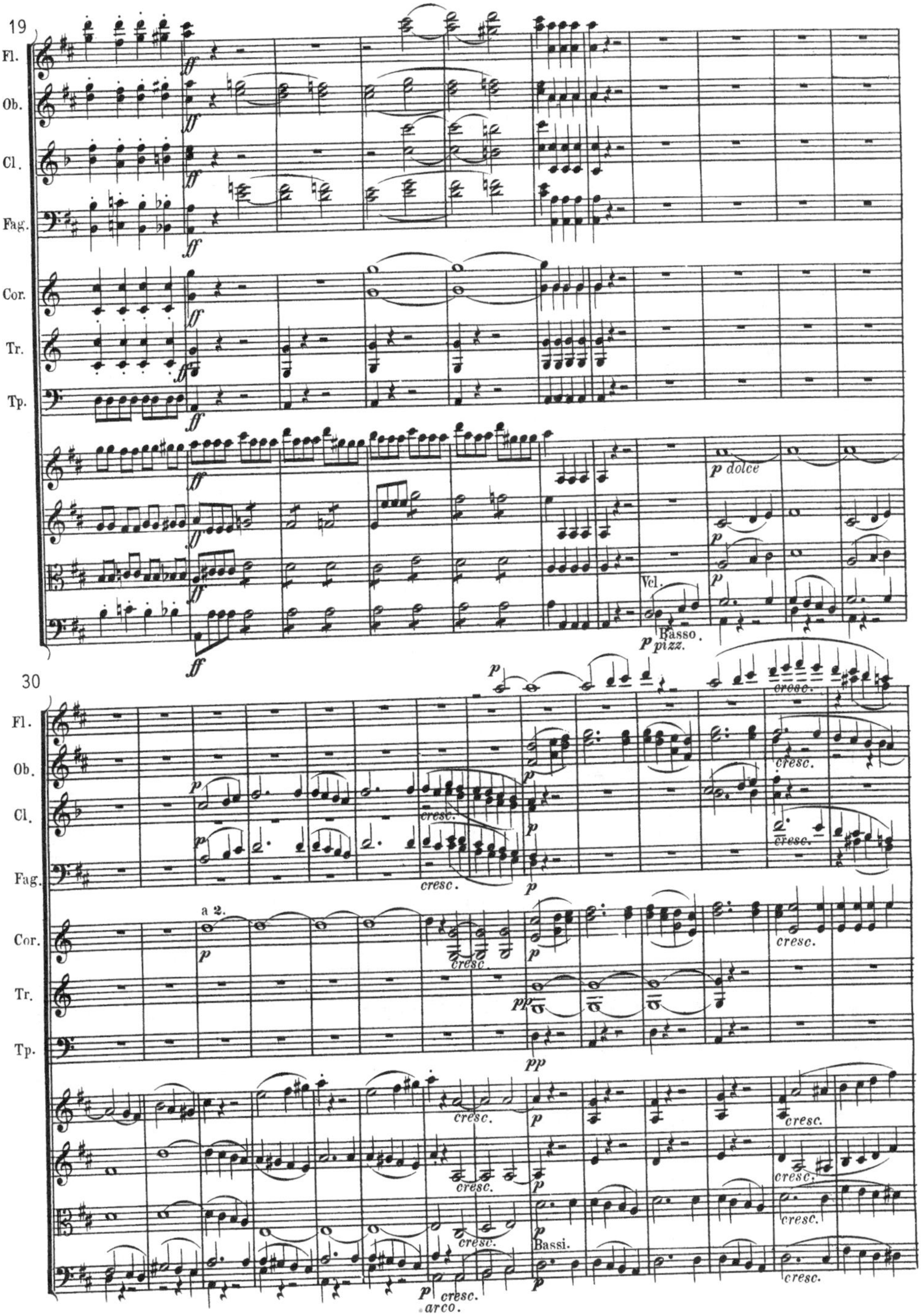
19
Fl.
Ob.
Cl.
Fag.
Cor.
Tr.
Tp.
ff
p dolce
Vcl.
Basso
p pizz.
30
a 2.
cresc.
pp
Bassi.
p arco.

44
Fl.
Ob.
Cl.
Fag.
Cor.
Tr.
53
Fl.
Ob.
Cl.
Fag.
Cor.
cresc.
decresc.

66
Fl.
Ob.
Cl.
Fag.
Cor.
cresc.
79
Fl.
Ob.
Cl.
Fag.
Cor.
Tr.
Tp.
a 2
cresc.

92
Fl.
Ob.
Cl.
Fag.
Cor.
Tr.
Tp.
a 2.
decresc.
p decresc.
104
Fl.
Ob.
Fag.
Cor.
cresc.
tr
Vcl.
Basso.

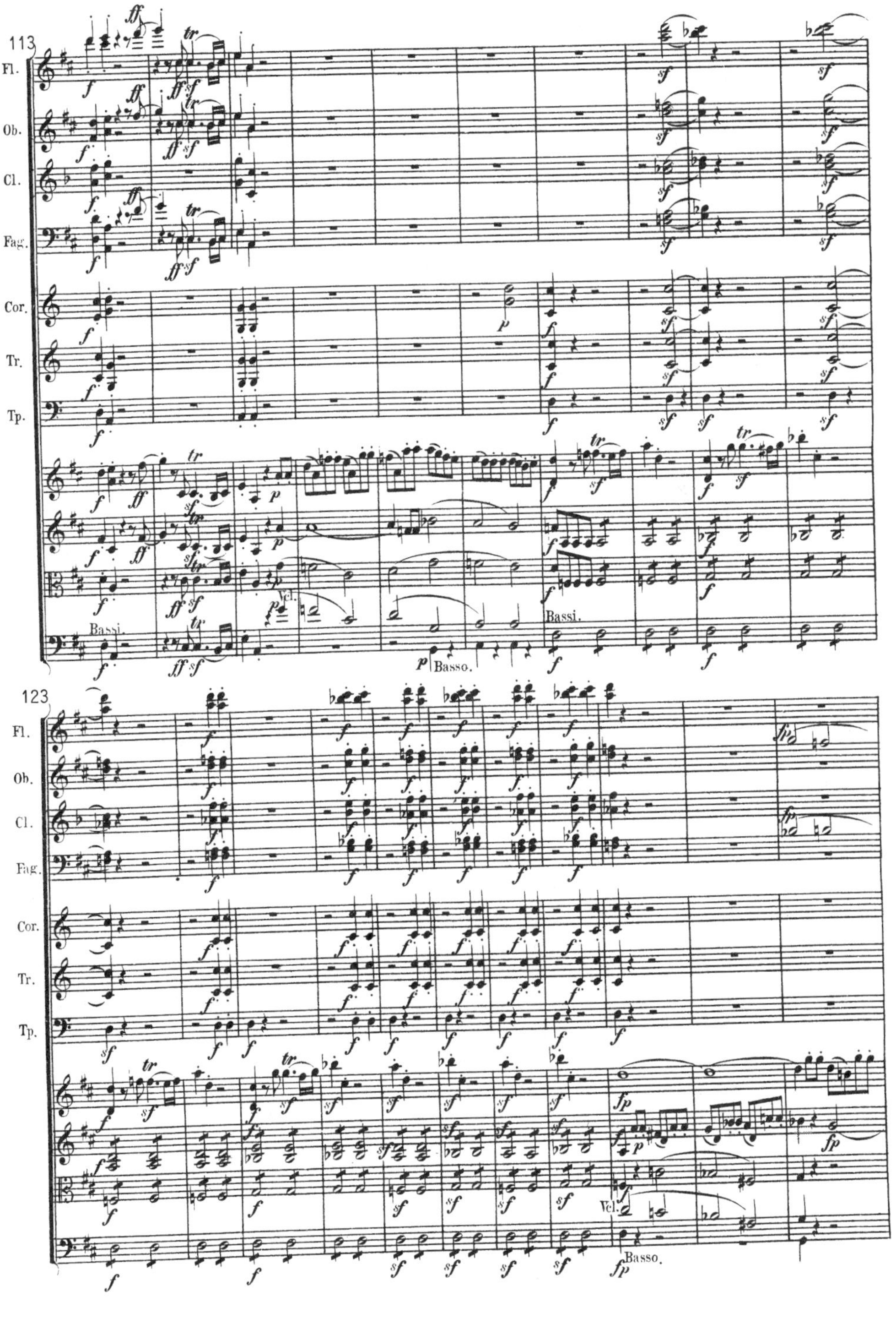
113
Fl.
Ob.
Cl.
Fag.
Cor.
Tr.
Tp.
Bassi.
Vcl.
Basso.
Bassi.
123
Fl.
Ob.
Cl.
Fag.
Cor.
Tr.
Tp.
Vcl.
Basso.

134
Fl.
Ob.
Fag.
Cor.
Tr.
Tp.
Bassi.
143
Fl.
Ob.
Fag.
Cor.
Tr.
cresc.

154
Fl.
Ob.
Fag.
a 2.
165
Cor.
Tr.
tr

174
Fl.
Ob.
Fag.
Cor.
Tr.
185
Fl.
Ob.
Cl.
Fag.
Cor.
Tr.
Tp.
Vcl.
Basso.
Bassi.
Vcl.
Basso.

195
Fl.
Ob.
Cl.
Fag.
Cor.
Tr.
Tp.
Bassi.
205
Fl.
Ob.
Cl.
Fag.
Cor.
Tr.
Tp.
p dolce.
Vcl.
Basso.
pizz.

217
Fl.
Ob.
Cl.
Fag.
Cor.
Tp.
cresc.
Bassi.
arco.
229
Fl.
Ob.
Cl.
Fag.
Cor.
Tr.
Tp.

239
Fl.
Ob.
Fag.
Cor.
sf
p
cresc.
decresc.
252
Cl.
Tr.
Tp.
pp

264
Fl.
Ob.
Cl.
Fag.
Cor.
Tr.
Tp.
cresc.
a.2.
276
decresc.

287
Fl.
Ob.
Fag.
Cor.
Vcl.
297
Fl.
Ob.
Cl.
Fag.
Cor.
Tr.
Tp.
Bassi.
Basso.

309
Fl.
Ob.
Cl.
Fag.
Cor.
Tr.
Tp.
Vcl.
Basso.
320
p cresc.
Bassi.

331
Fl.
Ob.
Cl.
Fag.
Cor.
Tr.
Tp.
cresc.
345
Fl.
Ob.
Fag.
Cor.
pizz.
pizz.

356
Fl.
Ob.
Fag.
Cor.
decresc.
pp
p
arco.
372
Cl.
Tr.
Tp.
ff
sf

382
Fl.
Ob.
Cl.
Fag.
Cor.
Tr.
Tp.
a.2.
cresc.
391
a.2.

400
Fl.
Ob.
Cl.
Fag.
Cor.
Tr.
Tp.
p
tr
409
cresc.
f
ff
pp
pizz.

END OF EDITION